Threads & Fri
BOOK NINE

Chen the Center Fielder Learns Confidence

by Peter J. Mulry

Copyright © 2022 Peter J. Mulry. All rights reserved. Except for brief quotations for review purposes, no part of this book may be reproduced in any form without prior written permission from the author.

Published by:
Peter J Mulry Foundation

Contact the author:
peterjmulryfoundation.org
850-221-1045

Print - ISBN: ISBN 978-1-7358638-8-7

I would like to thank several people who made this book possible - Lou Maggio, KR Lombardia, Gary Ippolito and Andy Taylor. I would also like to thank Mario Garcia, my Guardian Angel who has been with me through this endeavor. A tip of the cap to all the sponsors for their financial support.

Thanks to all who have helped me on my journey.

One sunny summer day, Coach Threads came to the All-Star team and told them he had some exciting news to share. "This weekend we are going to host a baseball clinic for all the kids in town so they can learn how to play baseball."

Chen, the center fielder, thought that sounded like a fun event. He had gone to a clinic when he was much younger and met Coach Threads and some of his teammates there. "Do we get to go, Coach?"

"You're going to do much more than that." Coach Threads grinned. "You all are such a great team and know so much about baseball, I think it would be great if you took turns teaching the kids about the different positions on the team."

Teaching the kids? Chen didn't like that idea. His teammates, however, seemed excited.

"I can show them how to throw a curveball!" Pedro the pitcher said.

"I can show them how to catch every hit," Samantha the shortstop said.

Each of the All-Stars called out something they could teach at the clinic. Everyone except Chen.

After practice, Chen walked home with Louie. "You've been really quiet, Chen. What's wrong?"

"I'm just nervous about teaching the kids at the clinic," Chen said. "When I had to give a book report just before summer break, I was so nervous that I was shaking and I did a terrible job."

Louie shrugged. "I thought your book report was pretty good. I didn't notice you were nervous."

Just thinking about speaking in front of people again made Chen feel queasy. He didn't like to be the center of attention, especially in front of strangers.

He worried about it while he was at practice, he worried about it while he ate dinner, he worried about it before he went to sleep, and as soon as he woke up. By the time the day of the clinic arrived, Chen was so nervous he was afraid he would be sick.

"You'll do great," his mother said that morning as she made him pancakes for breakfast. "Just pretend you're on the field, playing a game. You always do well when it's game time."

Chen wasn't so sure. When he was on the field, he was part of a team. Today, he would be on his own, leading a workshop about the job of a center fielder.

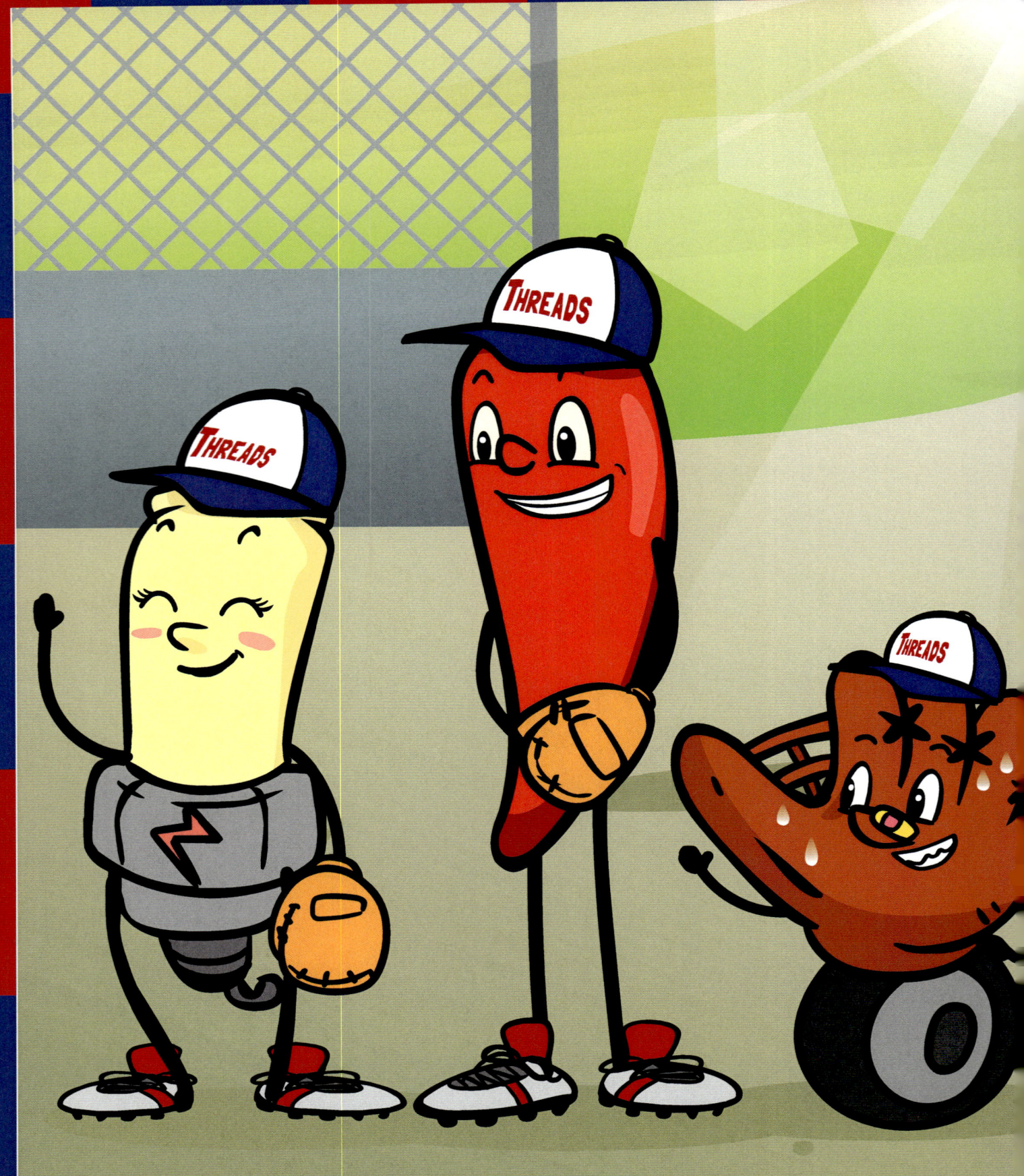

At the beginning of the clinic, Coach Threads introduced each of the All-Stars and what position they played. Pedro, Louie, Sam, Samantha, Gary, Cathy, Freddie, Rita, and Tony all waved and said hello to the crowd. When it was Chen's turn, he felt his face turn red. He gave a short wave, then hurried to stand behind the rest of the team.

Coach Threads divided all of the kids who had come to the clinic into different groups and sent them off with their All-Star teacher. There were twenty kids in Chen's group. As soon as Chen saw all those eyes looking at him, he started to get nervous again.

"Good luck with your group," Coach Threads said to Chen. " And remember, just be yourself."

Chen gulped and nodded. Coach Threads walked away and Chen turned to face the group. He opened his mouth to speak and...nothing. All his words seemed to get stuck in his throat. He tried again, but the nerves in his belly made him feel nauseous. He couldn't do this. He couldn't speak in front of others. "I'm sorry, everyone," Chen said, and then he turned and ran for the dugout.

Coach Threads found him there a couple minutes later and took a seat beside him on the bench. "What's the matter, Chen?"

Chen sighed. "I tried to talk to the kids, Coach, I really did. But I got so scared that I thought I was going to be sick and so..." He hung his head. "I ran in here."

Coach Threads looked out over the field where the other kids and the All-Stars were learning and practicing. "What's your job as the center fielder, Chen?"

"That's an easy question." Chen smiled. He loved playing center field. "I try to anticipate where the ball is going to go and be in the right spot to catch it. Then it's my job to throw it to the infield so they can tag the runner out."

"Exactly." Coach Threads gave him a thumbs-up. "To do that you have to be pretty confident, don't you? Because it's a lot of pressure to be ready to catch the ball and help your fellow outfielders."

Chen nodded. "When I first started playing on the All-Stars I was nervous about not being ready for the ball when I was supposed to be. Then I played a lot and all that practice made me not so nervous anymore."

Coach Threads pointed at the group of kids waiting for Chen to return and lead their workshop. "Do you think maybe the same thing could happen if you speak to those kids and share what you know?"

The whole idea of speaking in front of a group still made Chen nervous but he realized Coach was right. The more he did something that scared him, the easier it got, and the more confident he felt. "I'm going to go teach that workshop right now. Thanks, Coach!"

Chen ran across the field toward his group. He grabbed his mitt and a ball. Then, he took a deep breath and opened his mouth. "My name is Chen and I am the center fielder for the All-Stars," he said. His voice was shaky and his tummy was a little upset, but Chen kept talking. He could do this. "And I'm going to teach you all how to be the best center fielder ever."

The kids looked excited to learn and that made Chen even more confident. "You two, back up to the center of the field," Chen said. "I'm going to take turns throwing you the ball and teaching you how to catch it." He directed the other kids to take positions in the infield so they could be ready to catch whatever the center fielders threw to them.

"Let's pretend this one is a fly ball," Chen said. "If it comes at you and is going to land below your belly button, your glove should be down, like this." Chen put his glove low. "If the ball is coming in high, put your glove up, like this." He raised the glove above his head. "Now it's your turn."

He threw a few balls to the two kids in the middle of the field and had them throw to the ones in the infield. Then, Chen rotated the group so that every kid got a chance to play center field. As the kids learned to catch and throw, Chen talked to them about the importance of paying attention to the whole field and knowing where the other outfielders were. "We play as a team, which means we all need to work together."

One of the kids came up to Chen at the end of the workshop. He looked a little sad and there was a smudge of dirt on his cheek from when he fell down trying to catch a fly ball. "Thank you for the lesson," the other boy said. "I played terribly today. I don't think I'll ever get it and be a good ball player like you."

Chen knew that feeling and could see himself in that boy's eyes. "Everyone thinks that in the beginning. Why don't you and I stay after and practice? The more you do something, the better you get at it, and the more confident you will feel."

As the other kids began to go home and the clinic came to an end, Chen and the young boy played catch. The young boy missed several balls, but Chen was patient and gave him tips for how to hold his glove and keep an eye on the ball. Coach Threads stood on the sidelines and watched them playing. He was so proud of the job Chen was doing. And when Chen looked over to give Coach Threads a wave, Coach Threads gave Chen two very happy thumbs-up for a job well done.

Name:

Team:

Position:

Baseball Skills on the field:

Life Skills on the field:

Threads and his Friends is a look at "Life Skills" through Baseball shared by 10 Characters representing each baseball position on the field along with the Designated Hitter. I've always believed that most "Life Skills" are easily learned with the game of baseball.

"Life Skills" such as Responsibility, Accountability, Correct Choices, Commitment, Teamwork, Hard Work, Friendship, Confidence, Honesty, and Discipline, are all part of the tools we need to give to our youth so they can grow and prosper in the game of life. As I look at our young people today, I thought these characters might be fun for them while learning "Life Skills" and some basic fundamentals at each position.

Please have fun with it!!

I would also like to thank several people who made this book possible: Lou Maggio, KR Lombardia, Gary Ippolito and Andy Taylor. Also Mario Garcia who was my Guardian Angel in this endeavor and continues to be so. A tip of the cap to all the sponsors for their financial support.

Thanks to all who have helped me on my journey.

Peter J. Mulry

Pedro
the Pitcher

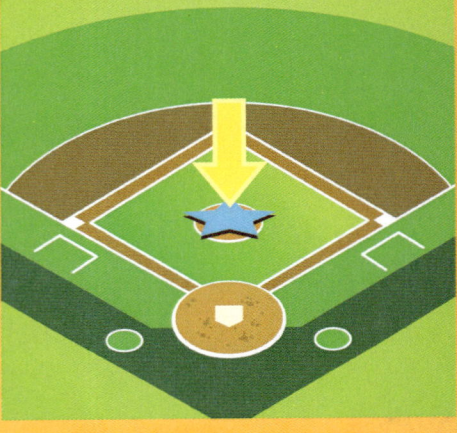

Pedro's Baseball Skills on the Field

☆ Learning how to get the right grip on a Baseball.

☆ Learning the strike zone.

☆ Learning how to get in the right position on the Pitcher's Mound.

☆ Learning wind up and proper throwing position.

☆ Learning how to pick up the Catcher's Target.

Pedro's Life Skills on the Field

Responsibility

Willingness - Pay attention to coaches.

Acceptance - Be a good teammate.

Responsive - Pay attention to all situations in a game and be alert.

Talent - Do your best and try your hardest.

Cathy
the Catcher

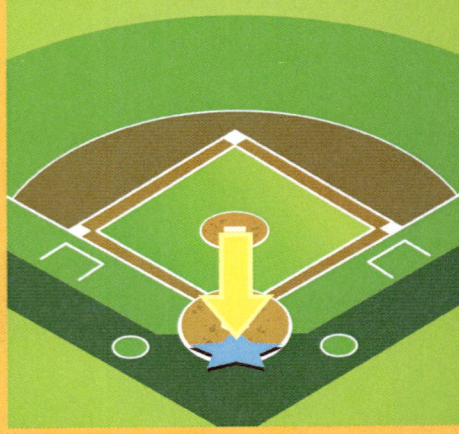

Cathy's Baseball Skills on the Field

☆ Learning how to put on the catcher's equipment.

☆ Learning the strike zone and where the target should go.

☆ Learning how to grip the ball.

☆ Telling teammates game situations and making her teammates aware of them.

Cathy's Life Skills on the Field

Accountability

Willingness - To learn the rules of how to play the game.

Accountability - Keeping herself and her teammates on the right track by being a leader.

Decision Making - Making the right choices.

Measurement - Knowing the rules. Knowing the count (balls, strikes, outs)

Freddie
the 1st Baseman

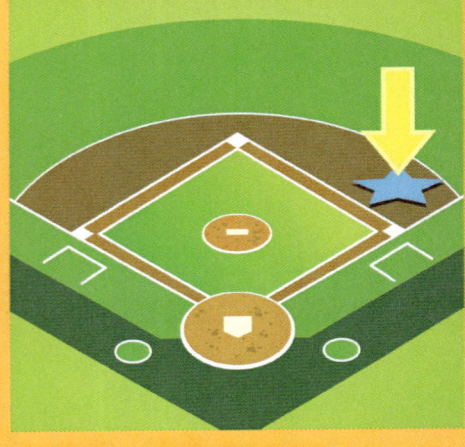

Freddie's Baseball Skills on the Field

☆ Knowing when a ground ball is hit to go to first base and put your heels on each corner of the base and be able to reach out for the ball.

☆ Learn how to use a first baseman's mitt. It will help make plays a regular glove can't—example a ball in the dirt coming from another infielder.

☆ Learning how to be the cut-off man for the balls hit to the outfield.

☆ Responsible for bunts on the right side of the field-when the situation calls for it.

Freddie's Life Skills on the Field

Correct Choices

Perception - Freddie learns by knowing what's going on every pitch during the game and what needs to be done.

Comprehension - Understand the game situation and pay attention.

Action - Taking the steps and making the choices to do what needs to be done on each play and doing it.

Manners - Know that there is a "Baseball Etiquette" when playing. "The Do's and Don'ts of the Game"

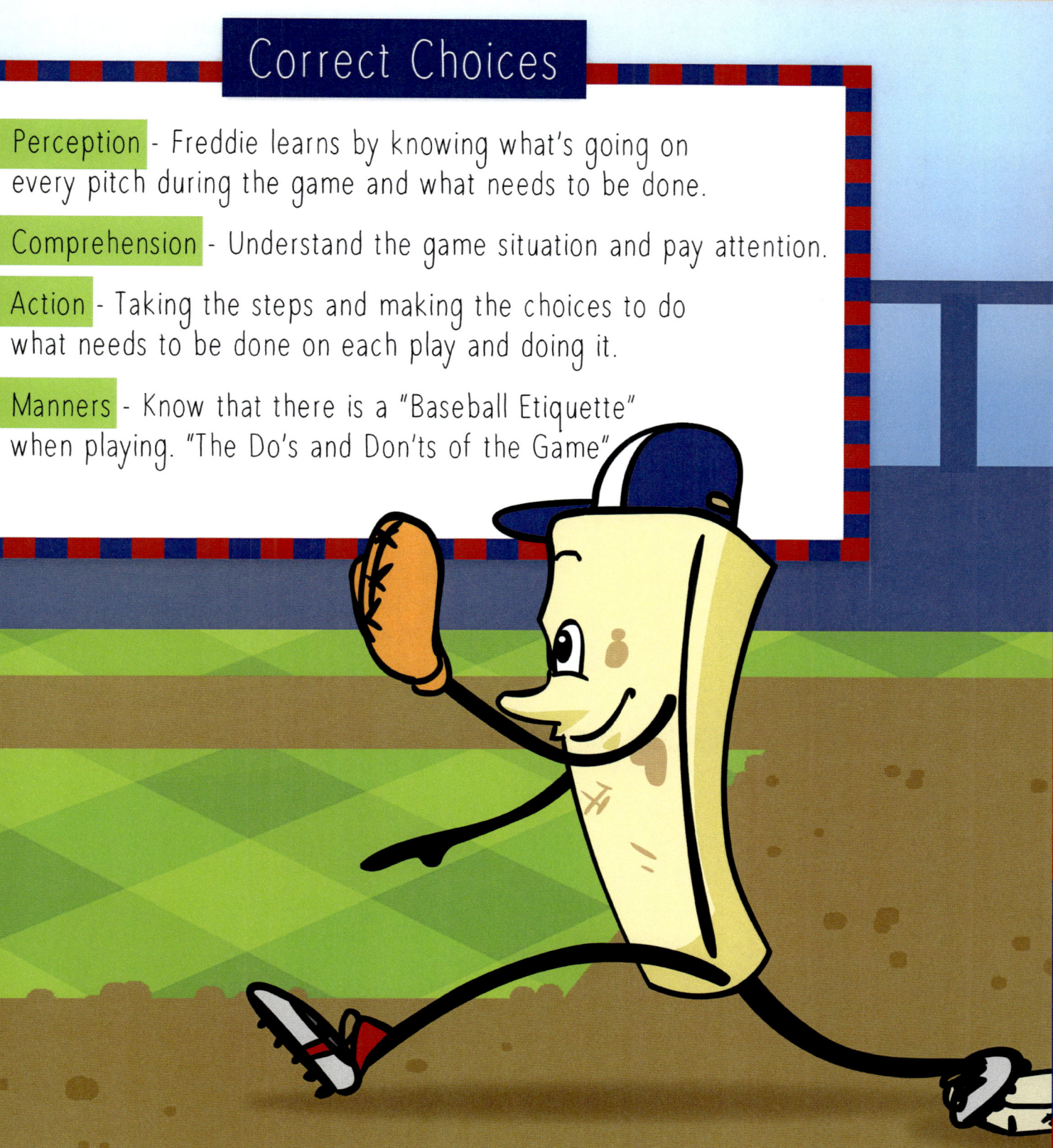

Sam
the 2nd Baseman

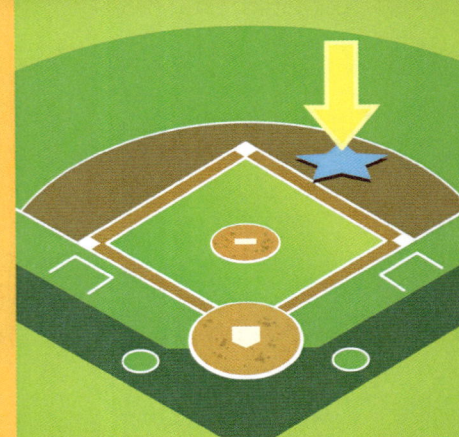

Sam's Baseball Skills on the Field

☆ Ground Balls hit to the 2nd baseman will go to first base.

☆ Ground balls hit to the shortstop or 3rd baseman with runners on 1st base-the 2nd baseman needs to go to second to get the throw for a force-out.

☆ In bunt plays he needs to cover first base-for the first baseman may need to field a bunt.

☆ Balls hit to the right side of the outfield—he will need to be the relay man.

Sam's Life Skills on the Field

Commitment

Conduct - Plays in a spirit of good sportsmanship.

Consistent - Belief of always giving his best on the field to himself and his team.

Sacrifice - Learning to take a little less to help one of his teammates.

Hustle - Never walk on and off the field without giving positive energy.

Samantha
the Shortstop

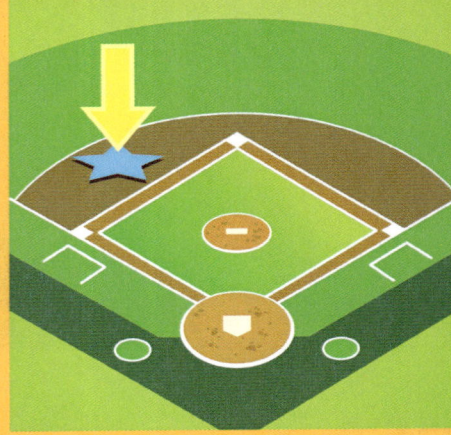

Samantha's Baseball Skills on the Field

☆ Needs the strongest throwing arm because she will make the longest throws in the infield.

☆ With a runner on first or second base and a round ball is hit to the right side she needs to cover 2nd base for a force out.

☆ In all bunt situations she needs to cover 2nd base for a possible force play.

☆ The shortstop is the relay person to the outfield from anywhere on the left side of the field.

Samantha's Life Skills on the Field

Attitude

Cooperation - She blends in with the team to get everyone to do their part. "She's a leader."

Common Goal - The common goal is to be the best we can with individuals working together to win as a team.

Respect - She knows that everyone has their own job to do and gives them encouragement to do that.

Selfless - Putting the team first-there is no "I" in team.

Gary

the 3rd Baseman

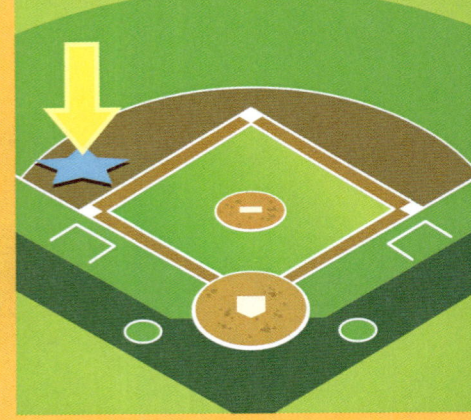

Gary's Baseball Skills on the Field

★ The third baseman needs to have quick reactions because ground balls get to him the quickest.

★ He needs to cover the left side on bunt plays.

★ With a runner on first base he needs to throw to second base on ground balls for a force out.

★ He is the relay man for balls hit into left with a runner on second base.

Gary's Life Skills on the Field

Hard Work

Discipline - Working hard every day on the field to become the best he can be. "Pay attention to the game."

Results - The end of game is determined by what you have done during the game.

Courage - Learn not to be afraid of the ball.

"Done is Never" - If you're going to be great at anything in your life you never stop working and getting better—catching ground balls every day.

Louie
the Left Fielder

Louie's Baseball Skills on the Field

☆ Learning to catch fly balls. The best way to do this is start by using a softer ball than regular baseball.

☆ Must learn how to throw the ball a longer distance for he will make strong throws back to the infield.

☆ Needs to be taught how to long toss.

　☆ His basic territory is from his position to the leftfield line.

　☆ Must learn with runners on base when the ball is hit to him which base he should throw to.

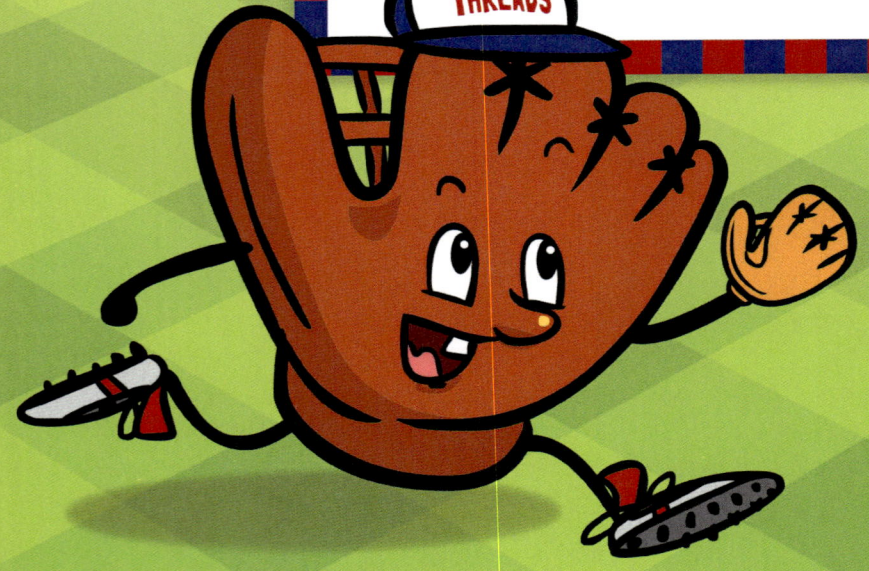

Louie's Life Skills on the Field

Friendship

Trust - Trusts his coaches and teammates to do the right things and make the right decisions so his team does well.

Honesty - Being truthful to his coaches and teammates. "Louie's always honest."

Connection - Getting close to his teammates who are part of a common goal. "Lifetime contacts"

Compassion - When teammates make a mistake or a wrong play he helps them with encouraging remarks.

Chen
the Center Fielder

Chen's Baseball Skills on the Field

☆ Since he has the best view of the hitter he needs to get a good jump on the ball and be ready to back up his fellow outfielders.

☆ Runs to a spot where he feels the ball will be—"anticipate"

☆ Catches fly balls with his glove up. Good rule to learn is if ball is below the belly button the glove is down. If ball is above the belly button the glove is up.

☆ Knows every situation when runners are on base so he knows where the ball should go.

Chen's Life Skills on the Field

Confidence

Purpose - Always a reason for every play made on a baseball field.

Expecting - Chen wants every ball hit to him—he knows his position and everyone else on the field and knows what to do!

Tenacious - He lets everyone know in the outfield what the situation is before each pitch—he is the leader in the outfield.

Study - Always wanting to learn and get better.

Rita
the Right Fielder

Rita's Baseball Skills on the Field

☆ Don't be afraid to go to one knee when a ground ball is hit to you.

☆ Be ready to cover all the way to the right field line.

☆ Back up balls hit to the centerfielder and the first baseman.

☆ Always be ready with runners on base if the ball is hit to us—which base are we throwing to-the right fielder is usually the outfielder who has the best arm.

Rita's Life Skills on the Field

Honesty

Truth - Being honest with herself and the situations around her.

Integrity - Don't cheat to win.

Sincere - Being honest.

Be true to yourself in the game, if it doesn't feel right tell your coaches.

Tony
the Hitter

Tony's Baseball Skills on the Field

☆ Get in an athletic position with your body—feet spread apart knees bent where you're balanced and comfortable.

☆ Put the bat on your shoulder pick it up and put it back. These two steps will help get you started.

☆ Work with a batting tee (all ages) to practice your swing—you need to swing the bat every day.

☆ Learn how to follow the ball from the pitcher's hand as quickly as you can.

Tony's Life Skills on the Field

Discipline

Instruction - Learning to listen to coaches and instructors how to hit and get into the right hitting position.

Repetition - Learning that to be good at anything you have to do it again and again the correct way.
"Perfect practice makes perfect."

Self Control - Knowing that anything worth doing takes time and you have to have patience with yourself.
"Don't get mad."

Practice - Is the only way to get better at anything we do. However doing the right things at practice is the key.

Coach's Corner
FINANCIAL AWARENESS

Financial Confidence

On the day of the event, Chen gets so nervous that he walked away from the group. Coach Threads reminded Chen that he knows his job as a center fielder well and he has what it takes to teach others. Chen was able to share his talents with the group of kids and help them understand that a team has to work together in order to be successful that team.

Financial confidence is an important skill to have as you grow up. In previous books, you set a financial goal. What route might you take to reach that goal?

Who can you trust to give you direction to help you meet your goals?

About the Author

Pete Mulry, one of the winningest coaches in high school baseball, coached for ten years at Tampa Catholic High School, and left that job with an overall high school record of 329-39. His team won State Championships in '68, '71, '73, and '76 and a National Championship in '73. He was honored as Florida Coach of  the year in 1968, 1971, 1973 and 1976 and Nominated for National Coach of the year in 1977. Pete then moved on to the collegiate level, coaching the University of Tampa from 1978 through 1982. He also scouted for KC. Royals. He was recently honored by the *Tampa Tribune* as one of the Top 50 coaches in athletics in the Tampa Bay area. He has dedicated his life, and his foundation, the Peter J. Mulry Foundation, to teach young children life skills through sports.

Look for the next book in this fun series!

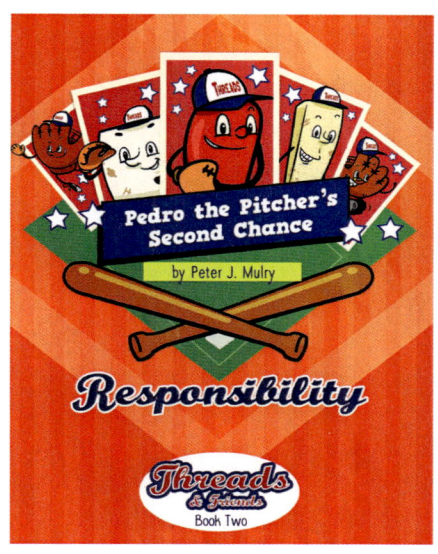
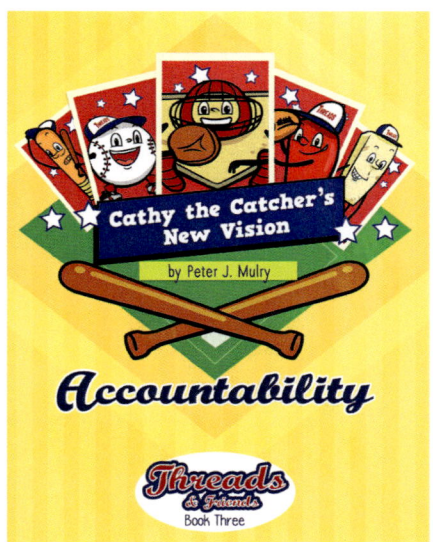
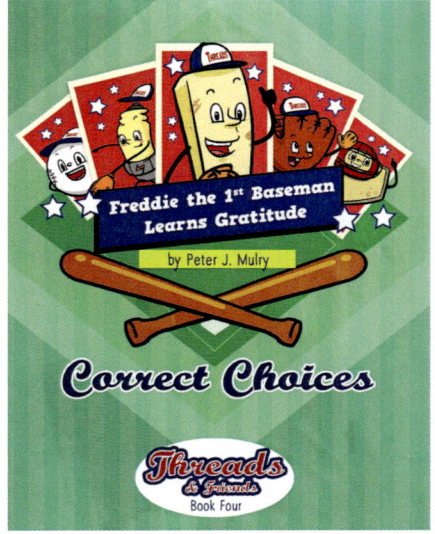

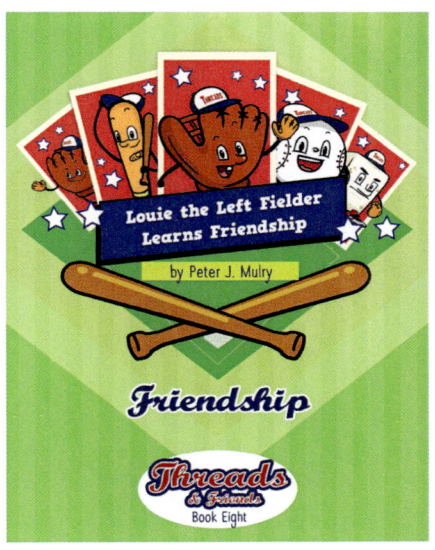

Made in the USA
Monee, IL
13 July 2025

20530116R00045